# BE A MAKER!

## Maker Projects for Kids Who Love

# DESIGNING COMMUNITIES

## MEGAN KOPP

Crabtree Publishing Company
www.crabtreebooks.com

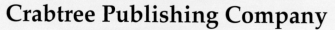

# Crabtree Publishing Company

## www.crabtreebooks.com

**Author:** Megan Kopp

**Series research and development:** Reagan Miller

**Editors:** Sarah Eason, and Philip Gebhardt

**Proofreader:** Wendy Scavuzzo

**Editorial director:** Kathy Middleton

**Design:** Paul Myerscough

**Layout:** Simon Borrough

**Cover design:** Paul Myerscough

**Photo research:** Rachel Blount

**Production coordinator and
    prepress technician:** Tammy McGarr

**Print coordinator:** Margaret Amy Salter

**Consultant:** Jennifer Turliuk, CEO MakerKids

Production coordinated by Calcium Creative

**Photo Credits:**

t=Top, bl=Bottom Left, br=Bottom Right

Library of Congress: Phil Stanziola: p. 9; Matternet: p. 15; Shutterstock: Aleksandr4300: p. 7; Andrey Popov: p. 24; Jillian Cain: p. 11; EQRoy: p. 18; Sarah Jessup: p. 19; Volodymyr Kyrylyuk: p. 10; Lazyllama: p. 23; Littleny: p. 5; Christian Mueller: p. 26; William Perugini: p. 16; Photo.ua: p. 6; Scanrail1: pp. 1, 4; Singkham: p. 22; Serdar Tibet: p. 8; Trabantos: p. 27; Tudor Photography: pp. 12–13, 20–21, 28–29; WHEDco: Chat Travieso: p. 17; Wikimedia Commons: Beyond My Ken: p. 25; Bruggenbouwer: p. 14.

Cover: Tudor Photography.

**Library and Archives Canada Cataloguing in Publication**

Kopp, Megan, author
        Maker projects for kids who love designing communities / Megan Kopp.

(Be a maker!)
Includes index.
Issued in print and electronic formats.
ISBN 978-0-7787-2879-5 (hardcover).--
ISBN 978-0-7787-2893-1 (softcover).--
ISBN 978-1-4271-1910-0 (HTML)

        1. City planning--Juvenile literature.  2. Communities--Juvenile literature.  I. Title.  II. Series: Be a maker!

HT166.K6575 2017          j307.1'16          C2016-907375-0
                                                              C2016-907376-9

**Library of Congress Cataloging-in-Publication Data**

Names: Kopp, Megan, author.
Title: Maker projects for kids who love designing communities / Megan Kopp.
Other titles: Be a maker!
Description: New York, New York : Crabtree Publishing Company, [2017] | Series: Be a maker! | Audience: Ages 10-14. | Audience: Grades 4 to 6. | Includes index.
Identifiers: LCCN 2016050630 (print) | LCCN 2016051290 (ebook) ISBN 9780778728795 (reinforced library binding) | ISBN 9780778728931 (pbk.) | ISBN 9781427119100 (Electronic HTML)
Subjects: LCSH: City planning--Juvenile literature. | Communities--Juvenile  literature.
Classification: LCC HT166 .K6575 2017 (print) | LCC HT166 (ebook) | DDC 307.1/16--dc23
LC record available at https://lccn.loc.gov/2016050630

## Crabtree Publishing Company

www.crabtreebooks.com          1-800-387-7650

Printed in Canada/022017/CH20161214

**Published in Canada**
**Crabtree Publishing**
616 Welland Ave.
St. Catharines, Ontario
L2M 5V6

**Published in the United States**
**Crabtree Publishing**
PMB 59051
350 Fifth Avenue, 59th Floor
New York, New York 10118

**Published in the United Kingdom**
**Crabtree Publishing**
Maritime House
Basin Road North, Hove
BN41 1WR

**Published in Australia**
**Crabtree Publishing**
3 Charles Street
Coburg North
VIC, 3058

# CONTENTS

# BRINGING COMMUNITIES TOGETHER!

A community is a group of people who share something in common, such as living in the same town, village, or neighborhood. Communities share a sense of place, which is a strong, often emotional, connection to an area. Larger towns and cities can be made up of many different communities living within their **borders**.

Ancient cities often began to grow around marketplaces, places of worship, and public buildings, such as those found in Athens, Greece, and in Rome, Italy. Over time, plazas became the heart of many communities as places to gather. As factories and industries drew more and more people to an area, small communities grew into larger cities. Automobiles allowed people to move from crowded and polluted city centers into **suburbs**.

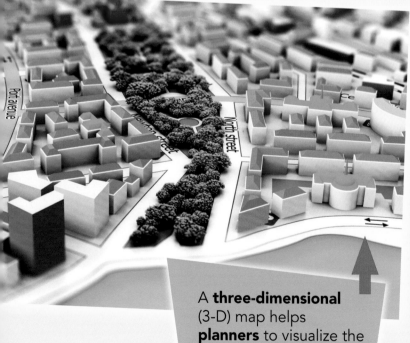

A **three-dimensional** (3-D) map helps **planners** to visualize the relationship between the different parts of a community.

Communities can be large or small. They usually include roads, open public areas such as parks, **public squares**, and playgrounds, **residential** areas, schools, and shopping areas. The cities and towns in which these communities are found are larger in scale. They may also include facilities such as factories, community centers, and government buildings such as city halls, libraries, and police and fire stations.

# WHAT IS A MAKER?

A maker is someone who questions. Makers are creative. Makers are builders. They look for ways to improve existing things or develop totally new things. A **makerspace** is a place where makers can come together to share ideas, learn, and create. Many communities have makerspaces in libraries, schools, and museums.

As long as there have been communities, there have been makers making things that other people needed. Today, the people who design communities are makers, too. Their jobs are to make sure a community works well for the people who live there.

Balancing open green spaces and high-rise buildings is an important part of community planning in **urban** areas.

## Be a Maker!

**Makers look at problems in their communities and work to find creative solutions. Today, many people live in urban areas where they do not have backyards. Starting a community garden gives people a public space where they can come together and grow food. Where could you start a garden in your neighborhood?**

# THE DESIGN OF A COMMUNITY

Communities are made up of parts. Most people look at a community and the first thing they see are the buildings—big ones, small ones, old, and new. Buildings help create a sense of place, but communities do not end there.

## SPACES IN PLACES

Within and around buildings are public spaces. These can include squares, parks, or neighborhood playgrounds. These are spaces where people meet up with other people, throw a ball, or enjoy art or music. Public spaces work well when they are well defined, yet flexible to the needs of the community. Planners must consider people of all ages, from young children to the elderly, and people of different abilities.

Union Square in San Francisco, California, has been a public space since 1850.

*SimCity,* **first introduced in 1989, was the original city-building game.** *Cities: Skylines* **came out in 2015. Like** *SimCity,* **it allows players to act as mayor and be responsible for public safety, to zone land for development, and to build streets,** power grids, **parks, and schools. If you had to design a city from scratch using a game, what elements would be most important to include? Why?**

## GETTING AROUND

Roads connect spaces and places, and allow people to move freely from one area to another. **Pedestrian** and cycle paths allow for more active travel. Some larger urban centers include rail and **subway** systems, too. Community design needs to make sure that everything is connected in a logical and effective way.

## PLANNING FOR YOUR COMMUNITY

It takes many people to design and build a community. Community planners work with the community to determine how it should grow. Environmental planners make sure that important natural features are protected. Transportation planners are involved with roads and highways, railroads, bike paths, and sidewalks. Other planners might focus on affordable housing, promoting businesses, creating jobs, or protecting historic buildings.

Planners determine where signs and signals are needed to keep pedestrians, cyclists, and motorists safe.

# IN THE ZONE

Within a community, there can be places to live, places to buy things, places where things are made, places for recreation, and places for community services. Traditionally, areas are divided into districts, based on their uses. There are shopping districts, **industrial** areas, recreational-use areas, and so on. These areas are also known as zones.

## COLOR ME HAPPY

Many planners use a color-coded map to show each type of land use. In one system, places where people live, or residential areas, are yellow. Places to shop, or **commercial** areas, are red. Government buildings, schools, and places of worship are blue. Places where things are made, or industrial areas, are purple. Public spaces and parks are green. Newer maps have more **mixed-use** areas. These are pink in color.

Some zone maps include symbols that show where certain **amenities** are, such as parking lots and hospitals.

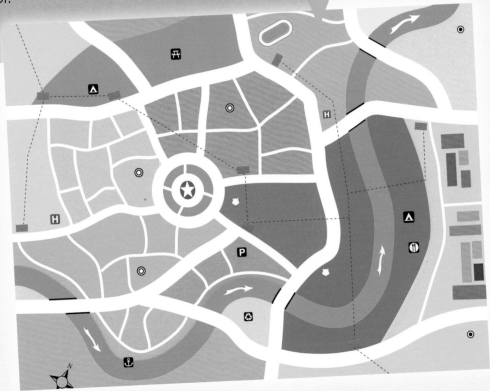

## MEGA-MAP

A geographic information system (GIS) is a computer system that planners use to compile different kinds of information on one map. This data can include the location of rivers, roads, and green spaces. It can show commercial, residential, and industrial areas. It can also show everything from sewer systems to power lines. Layers of information can be created with GIS. This allows planners to study how the different parts of a community relate to one another, all in one convenient program.

## MAKING IT WORK

Zoning helps planners design communities that meet the needs of its members. It keeps homes from being built near landfills and factories, and puts grocery stores near residential areas. Take a walk through your community. What colors do you think would appear on a zoning map? What colors seem to be missing? Why?

# Makers and Shakers

## Jane Jacobs

Jane Jacobs (1916–2006) watched how communities worked. She saw that it was important for people to feel connected to their communities. She believed it was important for people to have a say in how their neighborhoods developed. Jacobs wrote *The Death and Life of Great American Cities*. She was not a planner, but it was one of the most important planning books ever written. Jacobs encouraged people to become familiar with the places where they live, work, and play. She inspired the creation of Jane's Walks, which are free walking tours in local communities. Today, walks are held in more than 100 cities around the world every May—the month Jacobs was born.

Jane Jacobs worked to preserve unique neighborhoods in New York City and Toronto, Canada.

# A SPACE TO CALL HOME

Home is where the heart is—or so the saying goes! Homes are private spaces mixed in between and around community spaces. There are single-family homes and multi-family residences, which include **duplexes**, fourplexes, townhouses, high-rise apartment buildings, and **condominiums**.

## SPRAWLED OUT

In 1950, less than 30 percent of people lived in urban areas. After World War II, millions of soldiers returned home, got married, started families, but had nowhere to live except with their parents. Levitt and Sons saw an opportunity, and developed a new type of neighborhood on farmland in the state of New York. To meet the overwhelming demand, homes were mass-produced quickly and inexpensively. This marked the beginning of a housing boom in which affordable residential areas were constructed outside city centers. It was the start of communities growing outward instead of upward.

The term *tract housing* is used to describe a development of homes that are all built using the same basic design. It is also referred to as "cookie-cutter" housing.

Today, single-family homes are not normally built in city centers. These types of homes take up a lot of space. Property is valuable in city centers, and it makes more sense financially to build up instead of out. High-rise condos provide homes for many families. Open public spaces and parks are important places because many city dwellers do not have their own backyards.

# NEIGHBORLY DESIGN CHOICES

Planned communities today often include playgrounds for children, cycling and walking paths, and gathering spaces such as public squares or parks. Some new communities are reverting to back alleys, detached garages, and front porches to bring back a sense of neighborhood where residents sit out on the front stoop and say hello to people passing by.

Chicago's Riverwalk allows condo residents access to public space along the river.

## Be a Maker!

Take a walk around your neighborhood and sketch a map of the housing types. What types of homes are most common? Which ones are not found in your immediate neighborhood? In what ways does the housing work well? How would you improve it if you could redesign the neighborhood?

# MAKE IT!
# ZONE MAP

Our communities are made up of many different features. Designing community spaces involves many different people. Gather a group of friends or classmates, and tackle this mapping activity!

**YOU WILL NEED**
- Computer or tablet with Internet access
- Paper
- Pencils
- Ruler
- Scissors
- Colored pens
- Colored paper
- Glue

- With a group of friends, search online for a street map of your nearest town or city center. Or, if you can, visit your town or city center with a printout of a street map. Walk around and observe the different kinds of buildings and spaces.
- Take a look at the map and note where these types of buildings are:
  *Residential:* such as houses or apartments
  *Commercial:* such as stores or offices
  *Institutional:* such as schools, libraries, and hospitals
  *Industrial:* such as factories
  *Public or open space:* such as parks, public gardens, and town or city squares

**1**

**2**

- Now recreate the map of your town or city center on a large piece of paper. Include roads, and open spaces such as parks and squares.

- Create a legend for your map. Assign one color for each type of zone.

**3**

- Now it is time to begin your zone map!
- Cut out colored squares to represent the different kinds of buildings. For example, cut a red square for each residential building you observed. Using your map as a guide, glue the squares on the map to represent the different buildings. The different colored areas will show the zones in your community.

## Make It Even Better!

**Not only are there different types of uses, some communities have specialty districts such as a shopping district or historic district or ethnic district (such as Italian or Greek or Chinese). These can be mapped out and overlaid on your zone map. What does it tell you about the diversity of your community? Why not take it a step further and recreate your map using design software?**

## CONCLUSION

Take a look at the different zones. What patterns do you notice? Discuss with your friends how the locations of different types of buildings work well, and what is not as effective. How would you change the map if you could redesign the town or city center? Consider the relationships between buildings and their uses, such as where and why institutional buildings are placed in a certain area. What other type of information would be useful to include on your map?

# TALKING TRANSPORTATION

Transportation is a means of traveling from one place to another. It includes walking to the store, biking to your friend's house, riding the bus to school, or driving to a relative's home in the family car. Public transportation in large communities can include subways and trains. Transportation systems connect neighborhoods, communities, towns, and cities. Networks can be made up of roads, walking and cycling paths, cycling lanes on roads, and rail lines.

The Hovenring's design allows cyclists to ride on a suspended bridge above the roadway below.

## CREATIVE PLANNING

A big part of any community plan focuses on moving people around safely and efficiently. The Hovenring in Eindhoven, Netherlands, is putting forward thinking on the map. The **innovative** circular cycle bridge allows cyclists and car drivers to **commute** without the need to stop at a traffic light. Keeping traffic moving involves good community planning. What kind of transportation does your community have? What could be improved?

# MAKING THE FUTURE FANTASTIC

In the 1980s movie series, *Back to the Future*, Marty McFly rides a hoverboard and travels in a car fueled by food scraps. Transportation has changed over time as new technologies have been developed. In the future, we may have forms of transportation that do not exist today.

Designers and planners are always looking ahead. It is expected that self-driving cars will be on the road by 2021. They will be part of a ride-sharing program where several people share a single car.

## Be a Maker!

**Matternet is an innovative company working on delivery by drones. The drones can deliver small packages that weigh up to 2.2 pounds (1 kg) up to 12 miles (20 km) away. Imagine that one day all transportation, including that of humans, will be done with flying vehicles. What do you think a city free of roads and railways might look like?**

A Matternet drone does not require a pilot to fly. After a destination is entered using an app, the drone generates a route in 30 seconds, and then takes off!

# HIDDEN TREASURES

Communities have more going on than meets the eye. Water, sewer, phone, cable, and natural gas run beneath and beside roads. Empty spaces often lie below power lines, **overpasses**, and raised roadways. The question is: What can be done with the space above these pipes and below these structures?

## UNDER THE ELEVATED

New York City has run out of space—or has it? The city has millions of square feet of unused space under its bridges, highways, subway, and rail lines. These places are often dark, dirty, and not very appealing. The Design **Trust** and the New York City Department of Transportation (NYC DOT) are looking to **reclaim** and transform these public spaces.

The NYC transit system is the largest in North America. It includes more than 150 elevated stations.

The "Boogie Down Booth," part of New York City-based nonprofit WHEDco's mission to revitalize neighborhoods throughout the South Bronx, was a temporary installation in the Bronx. The Booth design concept was developed by Chat Travieso and Neil Donnelly for the Design Trust for Public Space. The project was so successful that two more booths were built in the community. Other ideas include **pop-up** community calendars where locals can post weekly events, developed corridors for walking and cycling, and places for farmers' markets and street fairs.

The Booth played the music of local artists 24 hours a day through solar-powered speakers.

# HOUSTON, WE HAVE A CISTERN

Houston built its **cistern** in 1926 to serve as the city's underground water **reservoir**. In 2007, the city closed the leaking structure for good. Four years later, Houston had plans to remove it completely, but designers took a closer look at it. With some creative funding, they have turned the space into a unique place to visit right near the edge of the newly restored Buffalo Bayou Park. People can walk around the cistern and view different public art exhibits. A **periscope** allows visitors to explore the cistern from above. With an adult's permission, look up the *Down Periscope* to take a peek inside the cistern yourself!

# Makers and Shakers

## Windmill Community Garden

In the Dutch Kills neighborhood of Long Island City, New York, local business owners teamed up with an art organization and a nearby school to turn an empty lot into a community garden. Together they have created a green space that includes a vegetable patch, colorful murals, places to sit back and relax, and a namesake wooden windmill. Students from the school care for the garden, while community members organize events, such as art exhibits, to showcase the talents of local artists.

# PLACEMAKING: PARKS AND PUBLIC SPACES

**Placemaking** is all about designing spaces that bring communities together. It inspires people to look at old spaces from new angles. Through imagination and innovation, public places can become the heart of a community.

## PROJECT FOR PUBLIC SPACES

The Project for Public Spaces (PPS) promotes building strong communities. Since 1975, the organization has helped create and maintain public spaces across the United States and in 43 other countries. PPS highlights important ideas for turning public spaces into vibrant community places. These include:

- Tapping into the talent and resources in the community.
- Looking at how a space is, or is not, being used and asking why.
- Having a vision.
- Starting small.
- Realizing that projects need to be maintained and updated over time.

Yarn bombing is a form of street art in which yarn is used to decorate trees, park benches, and other structures. The splashes of color liven up public spaces and showcase the talents of local community members.

# SKATE PARK, REVISITED

Riverside Skate Park in Manhattan, New York, is legendary. In 1995, the park was designed by teens. Twenty-four students worked with teachers and engineers to survey the space. They built scale models of the different ramps and other elements that the park would have. The design was a hit and the park was a popular spot in the community.

The park is now more than 20 years old. The NYC Department of Parks & Recreation released plans for a new, updated skate park. But skaters in the community were concerned that the redesign was missing vert, or vertical height, and that the bowls only reached 6 feet (2 m). They thought that the redesign did not meet the needs of the community. The skaters wanted to share their ideas for the redesigned park. So, they attended a local meeting to voice their concerns. Tapping into the community worked once. Why not try it again?

The skaters' plan worked. They met with the designer, and new plans were drawn up that reflected the needs of the skating community.

When designing a skate park, different ramps, rails, and bowls provide fun challenges for skaters of all skill levels.

## Be a Maker!

**Think about some of the shared spaces in your local community. How well do they serve people of different ages and interests? How could these spaces be improved or updated?**

# MAKE IT!
# MODEL PARK

Planners construct 3-D models to show how a design will look in real life. Step into the shoes of a planner and design your own model park!

## YOU WILL NEED
- A piece of thick cardboard
- Green construction paper
- Materials to build equipment, such as toilet paper rolls, straws, string, pipe cleaners, modeling clay, and construction paper
- Scissors
- Glue
- Grid paper
- Pencil
- Newspaper

**1**
- As a group, discuss what you want to include in your park design.
- Sketch a plan for your park on the grid paper. Will you have a separate playground area? Where would a bench work well? How might a pond add to the design?

**2**
- Cover your work surface with newspaper.
- Cover a piece of cardboard with green construction paper to look like the park base.

**3**
- Work together to make models of the different equipment on your plan, such as a tunnel, bench, and a swing set.
- When making your models, consider the scale, or the size each piece appears in comparison to another. For a pond, cut out a blue circle. For a basketball court, use a black rectangle.

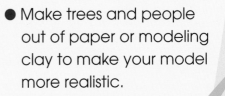

**4** ● Make trees and people out of paper or modeling clay to make your model more realistic.

**5** ● Following your plan, arrange the equipment on the board. Discuss the model with your friends. How well does the design use the space? What changes could be made to improve the park? Rearrange the pieces until you are happy with the layout.
● Once the design is finalized, glue the pieces in place.

## Make It Even Better!

Take your project one step further by recreating your 3-D model on a computer using a program such as *Minecraft*. Add more details, such as extra equipment. Visit the local town hall and ask for feedback from a professional planner.

## CONCLUSION

Take a look at your finished model. How well does it use scale? What other materials could you use to make your model even more realistic?

# MAKING THE GRADE

How walkable is your community? There are online companies that will rate your address for walkability from car-dependent to a walker's paradise. Vancouver, British Columbia, ranks as one of the most walkable cities in Canada. New York City, New York, tops the list in the United States.

In walkable communities, people can walk safely and easily. Goods and services are close by. Residents feel more connected. Neighbors are more likely to get to know each other. Studies show that houses are worth more in walkable neighborhoods. Walkability also leads to reduced crime, better health, and increased creativity.

## TEST YOUR NEIGHBORHOOD

Walk around your neighborhood and ask a few important questions: Are there sidewalks? Do they flow freely without barriers? Are they relatively trash-free? Are they wide enough for strollers and wheelchairs? Are there lights for nighttime use? Is there a grocery store, school, park, clinic, place of worship, restaurant, or an office building nearby? On a scale of 0 to 10, how would you rate your neighborhood? Why?

Many towns and cities organize walking tours to celebrate unique features of their neighborhoods. Stroll through your neighborhood and note interesting places. What appeals to you about these places? Why?

# TEST YOURSELF

How often do you walk or cycle around your neighborhood? Where do you walk or cycle? How safe do you feel traveling by foot or on a bicycle through your community? What could be improved to make your neighborhood more walkable or easier to cycle? How could you go about arranging a community cleanup for your neighborhood?

Designated lanes for walking, cycling, and driving keep people safe while on the move.

## Makers and Shakers

### Dylan Gentile

Dylan Gentile (born 2000) is not your average 15-year-old. He loves watching documentaries about public housing and reading books about walkability. He also plans projects to improve his local community. In 2015, the DeFuniak Springs, Florida, native founded Bike Walk DeFuniak. The organization leads projects such as adding sidewalks to improve pedestrian safety near schools, planting shade trees along local pathways, and adding signpost markers around town. His goal is to continue his education and get a degree in city planning.

# THINKING OUTSIDE THE BOX

Designing community spaces requires planning and creativity. New and interesting ideas can be met with astounding success. Sometimes communities need to look at things a little differently to make them work well.

## CHOO CHOO SCHOOL!

In the 1900s, children who lived in remote communities in Ontario, Canada and several prairie provinces did not go to average schools. The schools came to them on a railway car pulled by a train! The teacher lived in half of the car. The other half was the schoolroom. It had desks, blackboards, maps, and books. The school stayed in the community for eight to ten days, then moved on to the next town. After four to six weeks, the school returned.

## CREATIVITY IS IN THE AIR

Australia is huge. Some communities there are spread out over large distances. Until the 1950s, children had to go to boarding school or complete their lessons by mail. With School of the Air, kids could listen to lessons broadcast by radio. Today, lessons are sent by **satellite**. Instructors in studios use a video camera and electronic whiteboard to teach. Students can ask and answer questions with a web camera on their computers.

Technology allows people to connect over large distances.

# WORTH BOOKMARKING!

When most people think of a library, they picture a building filled with computers and shelves of books. In 2009, Todd Bol from Hudson, Wisconsin, started to think outside the box. He built a model of a one-room schoolhouse, filled it with books, and put it on a post in his front yard with a sign that read: Free Books. The concept was simple: borrow a book, then return it or leave another book. The idea caught on across the country and around the world. Little Free Libraries offer endless opportunities for creativity. Think about where you could set up a Little Free Library. How could you show your interests in your design? Visit the Little Free Library website to see if there are any locations in your neighborhood, and to find out more information on how to set up your own.

There are more than 50,000 little free libraries all over the world. Why do you think communities find this idea so appealing?

## Be a Maker!

**School grounds are not used in the summer months. How could this space be used for the community? What other spaces can you think of in your community that could be looked at in a different way?**

# KEEPING THE FUTURE IN MIND

Researchers predict that by 2025, the world will have 37 megacities. Megacities are urban areas with more than 10 million people. New York City alone will have more than 23 million people living in the area.

## SEEING THE FUTURE

It is hard at times to visualize what the future will look like. Take Portland, Oregon's Pearl District, for example. The area was nothing but railway yards and abandoned warehouses 20 years ago. Artists began turning warehouses into studios, planners began creating residential spaces, and stores opened onto newly created parks. Future plans are in the works to keep the area growing **sustainably** and creatively.

Market Hall is a combination of food market, recreation, residential, and parking areas all under one roof!

## DESIGNING FOR COMMUNITIES

Market Hall in Rotterdam, Netherlands, is a massive, arched building. Condos are built into the arch structure. Inside the arch, the open space is a marketplace where residents can buy fruits and vegetables. Japan's Yokohama International Passenger Terminal is a multi-use structure. It is a ferry terminal, a pier, a public park, and an event plaza. The design allows the terminal to blend seamlessly with neighboring parks.

# MODEL CITIZEN

Michael Chesko is not a planner, but he is a maker. Chesko spent more than 2,000 hours constructing a detailed, nearly perfect scale model of midtown Manhattan using only an X-Acto knife, a nail file, a Dremel tool, and lots of balsa wood. Chesko has been building little cities since he was a kid. Model cities are not just fun to build, they can be useful planning tools, too. A 6,500-square-foot (600-sq-m) model in Shanghai, China, shows what the city might look like in 2020.

The city model takes up a whole floor in the Shanghai Urban Planning Museum.

# Makers and Shakers

## Jason DaSilva

Technology can offer communities a whole new way to connect. Jason DaSilva (born 1978) has **multiple sclerosis** and is a **paraplegic**. Living in New York City, DaSilva was frustrated by the lack of information on accessibility in the community. So, he developed AXS Map—an app and website that allows community members to rank how wheelchair-accessible different places are in their communities. All over the world, AXS Map is creating more accessible communities in cities such as Tokyo, Japan, and Sydney, Australia.

# MAKE IT!

# MOBILE LIBRARY

Libraries are places where people access and share information and resources. Help spread knowledge in your community by making a mobile library!

**1**
- Choose a word or phrase to advertise your mobile library, such as "Read!" or "Read and Relax!"
- Use a pencil to draw the letters on construction paper.

**2**
- Carefully cut out the letters. Glue the letters on the white card stock. To make them waterproof, cover them with a sheet of clear contact paper or strips of clear packing tape. Cut the letters out. Leave a thin white border to make the sign easier to read.
- With adult supervision, use a hot glue gun to attach the letters to the storage container.

28

**3**

- In your notebook, draw five columns on each page. At the top of each column, write one heading: Book title, Date borrowed, Date returned, Name, Comments.
- Now think about where in your community you can set up your mobile library. Where do you think people will get the best use from your library? How about a local park? Be sure to ask permission before leaving your library in a public space.

**4**

- Gather any books you no longer want, and use them for your library. Ask your friends and family if they have any books they would like to donate to your project.
- Ask a friend to help you carry your library box and books to your reading area, along with a notebook and pen.

**5**

- Position your library and place the books, notebook, and pen inside.
- Every few days, check the notebook to see how many people in your community have visited your mobile library!

## Make It Even Better!

**Consider ways you can spread the word about your mobile library. What resources, other than books, could be shared in your community? Remember to think outside the box!**

## CONCLUSION

You did it! The library is finished. Take a look at your finished product. How well does your sign communicate the concept of borrowing books? Discuss with your friends whether any additions to the design are needed, and other locations where you can set up your library.

# GLOSSARY

**amenities** The features that make a place or building more useful

**borders** Outer edges

**cistern** A tank for storing water

**commercial** Related to the buying and selling of goods and services

**commute** To travel back and forth on a regular basis

**condominiums** Buildings that have manyunits where people live; they are usually owned by the people who live there

**drones** Aircraft that can fly without a pilot

**duplexes** Houses that are divided into two separate apartments

**industrial** A place where things are manufactured or built

**innovative** Introducing a new or improved way to do something

**makerspace** Where makers meet to share ideas, innovate, and invent

**mixed-use** Used for many different purposes

**multiple sclerosis** A disease which causes a person to slowly lose muscle control

**overpasses** Bridges on which cars or trains pass over other roads

**paraplegic** A person who suffers paralysis of the lower half of their body

**pedestrian** Someone who travels on foot

**periscope** A tube fitted with lenses and mirrors that allows a person to see something out of view

**placemaking** The approach to planning, designing, and managing public spaces

**planners** People involved in the development of a town or city

**pop-up** Intentionally opening, then closing within a short of time

**power grids** Networks that bring electricity from distant sources to individuals

**public squares** Open public areas that often have trees and places to sit, walk, and shop

**reclaim** To get use from something that has been used before

**reservoir** A place where a liquid, such as water, is stored

**residential** Referring to the places where people live

**satellite** A machine that is sent into space and orbits around Earth

**suburbs** Outlying residential areas of a city

**subway** A system of underground trains in a city

**sustainably** Done in a way that can be continued

**three-dimensional** Appearing to have three dimensions (height, width, and depth)

**trust** A group that oversees projects

**urban** Relating to cities and people who live in them

**zone** Officially saying a section of the town or city can be used for a particular purpose, such as housing

# LEARNING MORE

## BOOKS

Lyles, Brian, and Jason Lyles. *The LEGO Neighborhood Book: Build Your Own Town!* No Starch Press, 2014.

Reilly, Kathleen M. *CITIES: Discover How They Work with 25 Projects.* Nomad Press, 2014.

Steele, Philip. *A City Through Time.* DK Publishing, 2013.

Ventura, Piero. *Book of Cities.* Universe Publishing, 2009.

Yomtov, Nel. *Urban Planner.* Cherry Lake Publishing, 2015.

## WEBSITES

Connecting Dots shows the path from carpentry to city planning:
**www.connectdots.ca/community/building-great-cities-means-teaching-kids-build**

Future City is a competition as well as a website focusing on imagination, research, design, and building cities of the future:
**futurecity.org**

The American Planning Association presents a Q&A with different kinds of city planners:
**www.planning.org/kidsandcommunity/whatisplanning**

The American Planning Association challenges you to learn about where you live with a Neighborhood Scavenger Hunt:
**planning-org-uploaded-media.s3.amazonaws.com/document/Kids-Community-Neighborhood-Scavenger-Hunt.pdf**

# INDEX

## ABOUT THE AUTHOR

Megan Kopp is the author of more than 75 nonfiction books for kids. She loves her neighborhood's trails, and living close enough to walk or bike to the grocery store.